Buddhism for Beginners

No-nonsense Guide to True Self Discovery, Mindfulness and Developing a Zen Mind

Disclaimer Notice:

Please note the information contained within this document is for educational and entertainment purposes only. All effort has been executed to present accurate, up to date, and reliable, complete information. No warranties of any kind are declared or implied. Readers acknowledge that the author is not engaging in the rendering of legal, financial, medical or professional advice. The content within this book has been derived from various sources. Please consult a licensed professional before attempting any techniques outlined in this book.

By reading this document, the reader agrees that under no circumstances is the author responsible for any losses, direct or indirect, which are incurred as a result of the use of information contained within this document, including, but not limited to, — errors, omissions, or inaccuracies.

Table of Contents

Introduction

The path of enlightenment is supposed to take you away from the suffering in your life. Created by Siddhartha Gautama, better known as Buddha, around 2,600 years ago, this path is remembered by a famous cross-legged Buddhist statue. It's a path of everlasting peace, a way to become stress-free in a world full of chaos. It's a way to find love and happiness in a world that's full of heartaches and pain.

It was seeing people suffering for the first time when Buddha decided to find true liberation. Leaving not only his family but also his life of luxury behind, he traveled into the woods, where he started to find this liberation.

This book will not only briefly take you through Siddhartha's story on how he became known as Buddha but will also give you the basics of

Buddhism. With this book, Buddhism will become more than just the statue of Buddha in someone's garden. It will help lead you down your own path of enlightenment.

While you might feel you know absolutely nothing about Buddhism now, you will know more than you thought possible by the time you've finished reading this book. This book is meant to be a basic guide for you to start to understand Buddhism. This book will take you on a journey of learning such practices and beliefs as the three principle practices of the Buddhists path, the five basic precepts for any Buddhist, along with five additional ones for Buddhists who are learning to be monks and nuns. The book will also discuss the Four Noble Truths, the Eightfold Path, mindfulness meditation, karma, reincarnation, nirvana, Buddhism and science, and how we can use what we've learned in this book about

Buddhism in our everyday lives.

This book will explain the beliefs and practices of Buddhism and will work toward helping you start on your path to enlightenment. Through this book, you will learn the foundations of Buddhism, such as how compassion is one of the most important pieces of Buddhism or how you can work to have a clear mind through the beliefs and practices and meditation.

One important piece of information to remember before you begin your journey into this book is that everything you learn takes time and practice. This is also a strong belief in Buddhism. Just like the subtitle of this book states, through the chapters of this book, you will learn to practice the beliefs of Buddhism to help you live a stress-free life. Through the chapters of this book, you will be able to begin to find your ultimate wisdom, happiness, and love, which are exactly what the man who established Buddhism wanted everyone to find.

Chapter 1: The Buddha's Story

The man who became known as Buddha was born Siddhartha Gautama in Lumbini, Nepal, around 2,600 years ago. While the exact date of his birth has never been found, his story is one of the most famous inspirational stories in history. His father was the Shakya clan chief, who wouldn't let Siddhartha beyond the palace walls as a child because of the vision the Brahmins had over a decade before Siddhartha's birth. They stated that Siddhartha would become a great sage or universal monarch.

As a youth, Siddhartha was trained by the Brahmins for his future journey. He also learned archery, swordsmanship, running, wrestling, and swimming. When Siddhartha grew up and married Gopa, who gave birth to a son, people believed Siddhartha had everything. However, for Siddhartha, he felt something was missing.

Siddhartha wouldn't find his answer to what was missing from his life until he took his first trip outside of the palace walls. As he rode in a chariot around the city, he saw an old man, a sick man, and a corpse being dragged toward the burning grounds. In speaking to his charioteer about these terrible sights, the charioteer stated that people become sick, old, and die. Upon hearing these words, Siddhartha couldn't relax. He felt he needed to try to do something about these terrible events that occurred.

When he returned to the palace walls, Siddhartha noticed one more person. He saw an ascetic walking peacefully along the road.

He then realized his first step. He had to leave the palace and head somewhere where he could find the answer to help end the suffering of humanity. Quietly heading back into the palace, he said farewell to his wife and child, who was asleep. He then went into the forest, where he took his sword to cut his long hair. He then exchanged his clothing for a simple robe, which is usually worn by an ascetic.

Once on his journey for liberation, Siddhartha began learning from teachers who had taken the same path. After learning the technique of self-discipline, they asked Siddhartha to stay, but he felt he had to continue on his journey. For the next few years, Siddhartha and his five companions set out on a quest to find true liberation. But when Siddhartha changed by leaving asceticism and taking more food, his companions left him alone in the woods. He then became hungry until a woman by the name of Sujata offered him honey and milk, allowing Siddhartha to regain his strength.

Siddhartha then went to sit under the bodhi tree, on top of a mat of kusha grass, and crossed his legs. For six days, Siddhartha sat there thinking about everything he had learned and the texts he read. One day, he opened his eyes and came to the realization that everything he searched for never left. It was this day when Siddhartha truly found liberation and became Buddha.

Buddha lived his newfound liberations as the Awakened One in silence for seven weeks. Then the chief of the three thousand worlds, Brahma, asked Buddha to teach others about his liberations as so many were clouded. Buddha quickly agreed and began teaching others about true liberation.

Chapter 2: The Three Principle Practices of the Buddhist Path

The path of enlightenment has a few principles that are the foundation of Buddha's teachings. These principles are divided into three categories, which are *prajna, sila,* and *samadhi.*

Prajna

One of the first principles of the Buddhist path is prajna, also known as wisdom. Prajna is regarded as enlightenment, which is the main focus of Buddhism. When it comes to prajna, wisdom is a lot different than knowledge. Knowledge is what you know, a collection of facts. Wisdom comes out when you are most calm and pure. It's obtained through meditation and cultivation and comes at the end of your path.

Sila

The word *sila* translates to moral values and is important in the path's progress as it's the foundation of qualities. There are two principles that sila is based on, and these are the principles of reciprocity and equality. When the Buddhists speak of the principle of reciprocity, they are speaking about the golden rule: "Do unto others as you would have done to you." When Buddhists talk about the principle of equality, they are speaking about the equality of all living things, including the equality of security and happiness.

Samadhi

Samadhi translates to mediation. As a Buddhist, you want to obtain pure freedom, which you can do through mental development. You need to purify the mind, and the only way to do this is through meditation, or samadhi.

All three of these practices work together in order to purify the mind so that you can obtain complete freedom. You can't have one without the other.

Chapter 3: The Four Noble Truths

When Buddha started teaching about his enlightenment, he started with the Four Noble Truths. In these truths, Buddha is teaching about suffering, its cause, how there is an end to suffering, and what to do so you can end suffering.

Dukkha

Dukkha is the truth that states that suffering exists. Dukkha is real and universal, and there are several causes of suffering. Some of these causes are sickness, the impermanence of pleasure, and pain. Dukkha states that our suffering often starts because we have a desire that we can't fulfill.

No matter what we want, we continue to suffer because when we reach one goal, we want more. This is human nature, and Buddhists feel that in order to fully reach the path of enlightenment, we need to understand dukkha and take control of it so that we can control our suffering and take the next step toward entering the pure state of mind. An example of this is money. How often do we state that if we just had more money we could buy a nicer car or a bigger house? However, once we attain this level of wealth, we still want more money because we want more things.

Samudaya

Samudaya states that there is a cause for suffering, which is the desire to control things. Some people refer to this as the cravings or thirst for things that we can't have at the moment. There can be many forms of samudaya, such as the desire for fame, craving of sexual pleasures, and the desire to avoid unpleasant sensations, such as anger, jealousy, and fear. Buddhists also state that this craving creates karma, which is what makes you want more. When we suffer, we are ignoring karma because we are too worried about our own selfish desires and wishes.

When we let suffering take over, it's because we've let go of what really matters and started to focus on our wants. For instance, we start looking toward our neighbors to see what they have in life, and we begin to want that. We want the bigger car, the bigger house, and nicer clothes. We work on trying to impress others instead of focusing on compassion, understanding, keeping our minds clear, and karma. We also start blaming others for our own problems instead of looking inside ourselves to see if we can find an answer and cure for our problems.

In the eyes of Buddha, anything that made you unhappy or took away your peace was a cause of suffering. When the word *suffering* came to Buddha, it didn't just have to do with seeing people become sick, die, or get physically hurt. It also had to do with allowing ourselves to become unhappy, clouding our minds with unwelcome thoughts, such as "I have this, but it's not good enough, so now I want this."

Nirodha

Nirodha gives us the realization that there is an end to suffering, and this comes when we finally reach the liberation of nirvana. In Buddhism, the only true way to end suffering is to end your wants and wishes and your selfish desires. You need to become free of those thoughts. In order to do this, you need to understand the right view from the Eightfold Path. Only then will you be able to realize that suffering can end if we let go of what we want and find happiness within ourselves. Once this is attained, we let go of all the cravings we have and are truly free of our suffering.

Megga

Megga is the fourth Noble Truth, which states that the only way we can work toward ending our suffering is by following the Eightfold Path, or the Middle Path, which will be discussed later in this book. To end suffering, you need to follow a path. One of the best ways to understand this path of ending suffering, along with the Four Noble Truths, is to look at this as if you had an illness. For example, dukka is the diagnosis. This is the part where the doctor tells you what illness you have, and you come to realize that you have this illness. The next step of the process is finding the cause. What caused this illness? In other words, what caused this suffering that you've realized is inside of you? The third step, which is nirodha, is the treatment phase of the process. Now that you have observed you're suffering and you've found the cause, you can come up with a plan to help treat the suffering. The final phase, which is megga, is the recovery phase. This is the part where you've been able to get through the suffering and you're liberated.

Of course, it's important to realize and remember that no matter how hard we try, we can't get rid of suffering in the world. It's just part of life, and we need to learn to deal with it and, at times, overcome it. We suffer when we are born; we just have no remembrance of it. We also suffer when we are growing up and growing old. We also suffer because of death and other situations that happen in our lives, such as heartaches. Buddhism isn't about getting rid of suffering or finding ways so you don't have to feel like you are suffering; it's more about working to ease the suffering. Buddhism can work to try to give you an understanding of your suffering and why suffering exists in this world.

Chapter 4: The Five Precepts

In total, there are ten precepts; however, the first five are practiced by all Buddhists with the last five generally only practiced by those who are working toward a monastic life. These precepts are meant to help you achieve your highest status of awakening. These precepts are keys for Buddhists who are meditating so they can focus on their meditation with a clear mind and create a more simple daily routine.

Do Not Kill

The first precept is to refrain from taking the life of a living thing, including animals. When it comes to animals, Buddhists believe that it is worse to kill larger animals than smaller ones because the bigger the animal is, the more effort it takes to kill it. This precept is to help you focus on compassion, stating that no matter what, you should not harm a living thing even if it harms you.

There are five factors involved, a living thing, the perception of the living thing, the thought of killing the living being, the action of killing the living being, and the result, which is death.

There are also ways in which the action can be carried out. These ways include missiles, slow poisoning, psychic powers, sorcery, instigation, and one's own hands.

Do Not Steal

Buddhists want to keep themselves from stealing someone else's possessions. They also want to avoid such things as economic exploitation and fraud. This precept not only means that people should not steal items from their neighbor's house or a store, but it also includes not taking rides from a city bus for free. Not paying for your ride is the same as taking a possession that doesn't belong to you. This process involves five factors: (1) something belonging to someone else, (2) knowing the item belongs to someone else, (3) thinking of stealing the item, (4) the performance of the action, and (5) stealing as a result of the action.

Do Not Lie

Many people refer to the precept of "Do not lie" as "Don't gossip," "Don't call people names," and "Don't say anything false against anyone else." These offenses range from small to severe. A small offense would be a Buddhist telling someone that he doesn't have the item someone asked him for when the Buddhist has that item. A larger or more severe offense is to say you saw something when you didn't see the action, such as stating you saw your neighbor take someone's lawn ornament when in fact you have not seen him or her take it.

Like with the other precepts, there are four steps involved when it comes to lying. The first step is something which isn't so. The second step is thinking about deception. The third step is taking the effort to carry it out. The fourth step is actually stating this lie to someone else.

Do Not Misuse Sex

Misusing sex means different things to different groups of people. For instance, for monks and nuns, it means that they shouldn't engage in sexual acts. For people who are married, it means that they shouldn't commit adultery. Committing unlawful acts are also a part of misusing sex.

There are at least ten other groups of people, usually women, who shouldn't be a part of sexual activities due to unlawful nature. One of these groups consists of women who are bought with money, like prostitutes. Other groups include temporary wives, kept women, and women in war. Buddhists also believe that concubine women fall into the "misuse of sex" category if these women are being used for the fun of having sex, such as an extramarital affair.

Do Not Consume Alcohol or Other Drugs

The biggest reason why Buddhists believe you need to stay away from drugs and alcohol is that these are known to cloud the mind. In order to reach your full enlightenment, you need to have a clear mind. If your mind is clouded or you can't think clearly, you won't be able to obtain the clear mind you need to move down your path. While they don't consider prescription drugs to be part of this precept, they do consider social drinking to be a part of it.

Some Buddhists have even started to insist that other addictions can be considered drugs that cloud our minds—for example, addiction to our devices, such as computers, television, and smartphones. They state that these devices cloud our minds because they take us away from the reality of the world.

While many people don't feel that this precept will be helpful at first, after they have followed it for a while, they state that it helps them attain an amazing experience. People feel that their minds really do become clearer the more they keep away from drinking and any sort of drugs. They further state that they no longer find it strange or awkward to be one of the few people at social events who don't drink. People quickly come to realize that they won't be judged in any way if they keep from drinking even at a social level.

By not consuming drugs or alcohol, you don't corrupt your mind. Buddhists think of their minds as a sponge. Everything that you put into it, such as TV shows or video games, will corrupt your mind. Over time, this will begin to make you miserable because you have lost sight of what's really important as your mind has become cloudy.

Five Additional Activities for Certain Groups

Some people, such as those who are in the middle of preparing for monastic life or not within a family, need to add five more activities that they need to keep away from, along with the five precepts listed above. For Buddhists who are preparing for their lifestyle as monks and nuns, this is simply a means to help them attain the self-discipline they need within their monastic life.

Taking Untimely Meals

For Buddhists who are preparing for the monk and nun lifestyle, they can eat between dawn and noon, usually only a small meal or two. The reason behind this is that they need to learn self-discipline, and not eating during certain times allows them to focus more on meditation. Another reason for this is to help them avoid excessive eating, which usually occurs in the evening during supper.

Dancing, Singing, Music, Watching Grotesque Mime

While Buddhists prepare for the monastic life, they are not to engage in forms of entertainment, such as singing, dancing, watching TV, and music. These behaviors can lead to clouding the mind, which is something that all Buddhists are supposed to stay away from. By keeping away from anything that clouds the mind, Buddhists are more likely to be able to focus on their meditation and work on their self-discipline. Taking part in these types of entertainments can also give Buddhists certain senses that will make it hard for them to keep away from sexual pleasures.

Use of Garlands, Perfumes, and Personal Adornment

For this precept, you don't want to wear perfume, garlands, or any other type of personal adornment, such as makeup. Like when Buddhists keep away from such things as entertainment, they are keeping away from the use of perfumes and the like to help train the mind. The purpose of reaching your ultimate goal in your path of enlightenment is to keep a clear mind so you can focus on meditation and finding your inner peace. Another reason those aiming to enhance their self-discipline or preparing for the life of a nun or monk stay away from these items is that they can arouse senses that can lead to sexual pleasure.

Use of High Seats

This precept means that monks and nuns are to keep themselves at a level that is respectful for those who are above them. If they are to take high seats, it could boost their ego, and this won't help them in their path to enlightenment. They should not come to believe they are at a higher status.

Accepting Gold or Silver

This final precept ties into the previous one. Some Buddhists need to keep away from items that are gold and silver because these items are meant for people of higher status. By accepting gold and silver, they are letting in bad feelings within their body that can cause them to lose focus on their meditation and steer off their path of enlightenment.

It's important to remember that these precepts don't focus on whether you like something or not. They are put in place and practiced to help you stay on your path of enlightenment. They help you reach your true liberation, just as Buddha did. These precepts are placed because they have been known to help other Buddhists. They can help you keep a clear mind so that you can focus on meditation, which is a piece of this puzzle that will help you remain calm and find not only happiness but also wisdom. They aren't meant to directly test your limits on what you believe you can or can't do. They are here to help guide you. Everyone stumbles every now and then, and no one says that if you stumble on these precepts, specifically the first five, that you won't be able to continue on your path of enlightenment. These are here to help you build your self-discipline while on your path.

Chapter 5: The Eightfold Path

The Eightfold Path relates directly to the Four Noble Truths we previously discussed. Buddha created this path as he believed it helped him attain the state of nirvana, which is described as perfect peace. This path further helped him understand the natural truth of everything by erasing any delusions and attachments that were unhealthy for the path of enlightenment. In keeping with its name, the Eightfold Path contains eight pieces, all of which can help you advance on your path of enlightenment and find nirvana.

All eight pieces of the Eightfold Path are placed within three categories: (1) mental discipline or meditation, (2) moral conduct, and (3) wisdom.

The first two, right view and right resolve, are categorized into wisdom. The Eightfold Path starts with wisdom and insight because you need to understand why the path is important and why it should be followed. If you can't understand this, you will have trouble understanding the rest of the pieces, and then you won't be able to find your clear mind and liberation at the end of your path.

Right speech, right action, and right livelihood make up the second category of moral conduct. These three parts of the Eightfold Path together create a harmony that will help lead you further into the path so you can find your liberation.

Right effort, right mindfulness, and right concentration create the first category of mental discipline or meditation. These are the steps along the Eightfold Path that will help bring you to the end and help you find liberation. In these steps, you will have a clear mind and be able to understand situations around you.

Right View

Right view includes the Four Noble Truths and how we should value them for our soul, mind, and body. It speaks about the cycle of rebirth and karma with how we should interpret these terms within the Buddhist religion. By completely understanding the Four Noble Truths, the cycle of rebirth, and karma, you are able to keep your mind clear from cloudy thoughts as these pieces of Buddhism help you think clearly. Once you understand these pieces, you have the right view. In a sense, the right view is how you perceive the world. It's also how your perception of the world affects your actions and thoughts.

In Buddhism, the cycle of rebirth discusses how, after people die, they are sent to a place called Bardo. In Bardo, they are able to decide who they should be in their next life. Buddhists also feel that the closer you are to your enlightenment, the more clearly you will be able to see who you could become in Bardo. If your mind is cloudy, you will have a difficult choice because you won't be able to see your future self clearly.

Right Resolve

This piece of the Eightfold Path is also referred to as the right thought or right intention. Right resolve is the piece that teaches you to stop and think before you act on something. For instance, if you're out in a grocery store and you hear someone gossiping about your friend, how you act will determine if you have the right resolve or not. If you have the right resolve, you're going to think about all the pieces of the situation and not just yourself and what you heard about your friend. If you act in the right resolve, you will realize what the right action is.

When you have the right resolve, you will have compassion and understanding over wishing someone ill will. Even when you don't believe in that person's actions, you will come to understand the situation and continue to have compassion for the person.

Right Speech

Right speech is exactly as it sounds. It's about using kind, understanding, and compassionate words over hateful words. In Buddhism, you always want to be peaceful. If you find it in your heart to cause harm or hate someone for whatever they did or said, you're not liberated, you don't understand the Four Noble Truths, and you're not on your way to the right speech. When people are suffering or angry, they often state things that are hurtful toward another person. In order to end the suffering and keep the suffering away, you need to say kind words.

Right Action

Right action, which is also known as the right virtue, is the piece of the Eightfold Path that respects the five precepts and keeps a person away from violence. This means you don't kill or harm another living being, you don't misuse sex, and you follow all the other precepts that we previously talked about, including the five additional precepts for monks and nuns.

Right Livelihood

Right Livelihood is your right to live a happy and fulfilling life. But in order to do this, you have to stay away from the selfish wishes and desires that will make you unhappy. If you work, you do so in a way where you won't harm anyone else or yourself.

Right Effort

With right effort, you want to take action, but do so in a way that you respect the five or ten precepts, depending on how many of them you have to follow. For example, if you're in a store and you hear someone gossiping negatively about your friend, you can react, but you have to do so in a way that you don't harm yourself, your friend, or anyone else involved.

Right Mindfulness

In right mindfulness, you are totally aware of your surroundings, yourself, and others. Not only are you aware of the precepts and the Four Noble Truths, but you also take into consideration the seven factors of awakening. These seven factors are mindfulness, investigation of reality's nature, energy, joy, relaxation, clear awareness, and equanimity.

Right Concentration

Right concentration (right samadhi) brings you a deep understanding of peace and unity between your mind, body, and soul.

Once you follow the Eightfold Path, you will reach a level of maturity in which you attain high wisdom and understanding of nature and its existence along with yours. At this point, it's believed that you have reached an unshakable liberation, which can further allow you deeper experience and insight into future situations.

Chapter 6: Karma, Reincarnation, and Nirvana

Buddhists hold many center beliefs. Three of these beliefs are karma, reincarnation, and nirvana.

Karma

For Buddhists, the theory of karma is the center of their beliefs. For Buddhists, karma is the state of mind that comes before the action. Buddhists also believe in karma law. This law states that karma is essentially a cause-and-effect relationship. This means that if you have a good cause, the effect will be good; and if you have a bad cause, the effect will be bad.

You might have noticed by now that Buddhists have a different definition for karma than what you might be used to. Before we get into the truths Buddhists believe about karma, we should discuss the falsehoods many people believe about karma.

False Karma

A false belief about karma to Buddhists is that if someone is poor, they must stay poor because this is their karma. Buddhists want the best for people, not just themselves. They want to see people live a happy and peaceful life. While they don't follow the life of the rich, they want people to be well taken care of and happy. An exclusion to this rule is if someone who lives in poor conditions chooses to do so on his own free will. If a person chooses to live in poor conditions, then Buddhists will not try to take better care of this person because the person wants the life they're living.

Some people believe that people suffer because it's their karma. A Buddhist would never feel this way because they don't want to see people suffer. While they believe that karma can have a negative cause-and-effect relationship, they have compassion and understanding and generally help if someone is in need of help.

Finally, people believe that those who are rich are better off than those who aren't because people who are rich have good karma. Once again, Buddhists don't strive to have the riches in the world; they strive to live a life of peace and happiness and don't want what others have. According to the Buddhist meaning of cause and effect, this wouldn't be in the category of karma. To a Buddhist, this belief is false karma.

True Karma

When you're learning about Buddhism, it's important to understand the truths they believe about karma over the fallacies. For Buddhists, there are four truths of karma just like there were four falsehoods of karma.

First, we can change the power of karma because it's within us. When some people talk about karma, they believe that it can't be changed because it comes from our actions. While Buddhists feel that karma comes from actions, they also believe karma can change because it's not a fate that floats around trying to get revenge against some people. It's inside all of us, and this gives us the power to change it.

Second, Buddhists believe that since karma is inside of us, we have to do whatever we can to eliminate the suffering of others. It's our responsibility to do what we can to make the world a better and happier place for everyone. This stems from the first time Buddha left the walls of his castle and received an introduction to suffering. The reason why he went into the woods to find his liberation was he wanted to try to help people so they didn't have to suffer in their daily lives.

Third, Buddhists believe that the best karma you can have within yourself is compassion. Compassion is a central goal within Buddhism, and if you have found your compassion and you can share it with others, you are on your right path toward enlightenment. Compassion can help us understand the suffering people have inside of themselves, which is often why they say things that are negative or act in a negative way. In a simple sense, Buddhists don't believe in "An eye for an eye," and they don't believe in getting revenge. They feel that the best revenge is to simply be compassionate to people as this can help release some of their sufferings, and they too might be able to head toward the path of enlightenment.

Finally, Buddhists realize that everyone can be subject to bad karma. We're not perfect; we are human beings. We make mistakes. We say things we don't mean. We don't always follow the path of enlightenment as we should. However, if you sway off your path a little or if you see someone who is in bad karma, you can change this by embracing good karma. I've said it before, and I'll say it again because it's a central point for karma in Buddhism: Karma is within all of us, and we have the power to change it. Therefore, if you feel bad karma, you can work on changing it for good karma.

Reincarnation

Of course, with Buddha bringing out Buddhism around 2,600 years ago, things have changed a bit over time. While many beliefs remain the same, such as the Four Noble Truths and the Eightfold Plan, some things have gained a more modern explanation than the one Buddha discussed. An example of this is reincarnation and rebirth. For modern-day Buddhists, these two works often go hand in hand. Some say they don't believe in reincarnation because it doesn't exist; instead, they believe in rebirth. Others use the terms interchangeably, and there are also those who believe in both.

Because this is a book of Buddhism for beginners, I don't want to focus too much on the differences between reincarnation and rebirth. Instead, I will focus on reincarnation as this is the more modern usage, especially in the

Western world, for Buddhists. When you pick up other books about Buddhism, chances are they will discuss reincarnation. Once you have a better grip on Buddhism, you can decide for yourself whether you more likely follow the path of reincarnation or rebirth or if they are the same term.

In Buddhism, karma and reincarnation (or rebirth, as some books say) go hand in hand. A way to look at this is saying that karma begets karma, which is the core of reincarnation. What this means is that as long as you have good karma within you, you'll continue to have good karma within your life. Then after death, you will have good karma within nature. This good karma will last forever or until you hold bad karma, which will interrupt the good karma. However, because karma is inside of you, you can easily return the good karma.

Another way to look at the relationship between karma and reincarnation is the following: If you have good karma in your life, when you are reborn (this is often why the word *rebirth* comes into play), you will continue to have good karma. This will continue no matter how many times you go through the reincarnation process unless you hold bad karma. If you carry this bad karma in you during your reborn process, you will continue to have bad karma. This will last until you start to hold good karma within you.

When people usually think of reincarnation, they think of the soul transferring from one body to the next. While many Buddhists believe that you do go from one life to the other—sometimes you live as an animal and sometimes as a human—they don't believe that the soul remains whole, which might be something you have been taught. Instead,

Buddhists believe that you are in tune with nature as a human being is just a person with a collection of thoughts, emotions, and awareness. These are sent to nature, and then nature sends them back, which is how you continue to receive good karma or bad karma, depending on your thoughts and actions. Once nature sends you back, then you have been reborn or reincarnated.

For someone who is just learning about Buddhism, a lot of the beliefs and practices can be confusing at first. However, you will quickly catch on the more you study Buddhism. As long as you remember the core beliefs, such as the Eightfold Path, the Four Noble Truths, compassion, keeping a clear head, and other beliefs and practices we have discussed, you'll quickly catch on to Buddhism. By now, you should have an idea of the major beliefs of Buddhism. If you don't fully understand all of them, don't worry as you will in time.

Now, let's continue to learn a bit more about reincarnation. Within reincarnation, Buddhists believe there are ten realms of being, which are ten conditions we deal with in our lives every day. These ten realms of being are broken down into two groups. The first group is known as the four higher realms of nobility, and the second group is known as the six realms of desire. I will further explain the two groups below.

Six Realms of Desire

Naraka (hell) is the first realm of desire. Once you get to this realm, it is nearly impossible to escape. Even if you do, it takes a lot of time and patience. People who are in this realm literally feel trapped. They mainly hold negative feelings of anger, hostility, and frustration. They are often violent as they don't know how else to let go of their anger. People who are trapped in this realm always feel they have to destroy those around them, and then, in response, they destroy themselves.

Pretas (hunger), often called the world of hungry ghosts, is the next realm of desire. When Buddhists talk about hunger in this realm, they don't literally mean people feel hungry for food. They mean that people feel hungry for more possessions, whether it's another car, a bigger house, or more money. They have a desire to own as much as possible. People in this realm are never satisfied with what they have and always feel that other people have more or better possessions and they want to have the best.

People in this realm don't care about other individuals. They are selfish and only care about themselves and their desires. It's very hard for people in this realm to learn the technique of self-discipline, which is a big part of Buddhism and something you need in order to complete meditation and find your liberation. While people in this realm have an easier time getting out, once they realize their thoughts and actions, it's still hard for them to crawl out of this realm. However, it has been and can be accomplished.

The *animal realm* is the third realm of desire, and it is sometimes referred to as the world of animals because of how people act within this realm. People trapped in this realm don't have a sense of morality and tend to think and act based on instincts, which is what animals are known to do. Because of this, they also often don't have reasoning for their actions. They don't think of their actions; they just act.

People in the realm of brutality often manipulate and use people for their own selfish reasons. They don't think and sometimes don't care how this affects other people. People can come out of this realm once they realize their thoughts and actions and start to change. While it's a lot of work and a lot of learning on their part, once they reach their destination, they have a better chance of finding their liberation.

The fourth realm of desire is *arrogance.* In this modern world, this is probably one of the realms people can most relate to. When you think of an arrogant being, he or she will fit into this realm. They are the people who, while they care about others, are more worried about themselves, how they look to the outside world, what they have, and how often they can win. They not only think they can be the best, but they know they are the best. While most people might see this as a positive personality trait, it goes against what Buddha taught and what Buddhists still continue to believe. The person in this realm is often run on jealousy, especially if they aren't the best, and they have been known to harm people over their jealousy. Because people in the arrogant realm are so competitive and jealous, they tend to lack compassion, and their minds are clouded with their selfish desires.

Passionate idealism is what Buddhists call the fifth realm of desire. The people of this realm are often considered perfectionists. While this can be a good desire, as it can lead a person to go toward their path of enlightenment, it's generally used as a negative desire because of the way they tend to act when things aren't perfect and the way people tend to view them. People in this realm are often thought to be very critical because they want everything to be perfect. They are also very self-critical, which is usually what stops them from being able to reach their liberation. Buddhists believe that in order for perfectionists to achieve their full liberation, they have to be able to let go of their imperfections, which is an extremely hard thing for a perfectionist to accomplish. But it's not impossible.

Heaven realm, or rapture, is the sixth and final realm of desire. Buddhists categorize people who have brief periods where they get pure pleasure. This is the easiest realm of desire to get out of, and the periods are often very short. After they have their moment in the heaven realm, they then come back to one of the realms of nobility.

Four Higher Realms of Nobility

For Buddhists, the higher realms of nobility are the ones they want to use so they can work toward their path of enlightenment.

The first one for the higher realm of nobility (seventh out of all ten realms) is *learning*. Also known as the realm of the enlightened disciples of Buddha. It consists of people who are in the learning phase of Buddhism, such as you reading this book. They are interested in learning about Buddhism. They want to learn more about Buddhist practices and beliefs, such as the Eightfold Path and the core beliefs. The people of this realm work to learn about Buddhism so they can work toward their path of enlightenment.

People in this realm will often look for a mentor, who is called a guru, so they can better understand the beliefs and practices of Buddhism. If they can't find guidance through the help of a mentor, then they continue to learn about Buddhism through books and other means, which in today's world can mean certain webpages on the internet.

Because some of you are in this realm, I will spend a little more time on it than the other realms. People in this realm can continue to work their way up toward other realms, providing they keep an open mind about what they are learning. Sometimes, especially when you grow up learning another faith, it can be hard to open your mind to things that are being taught. However, if you remember to keep an open mind and desire a willingness to learn, you'll be able to move into the next realm and closer to your enlightenment without too much of a problem.

Absorption is the second realm of nobility and the eighth realm overall. This realm, which is also referred to as Pratyekabuddha (meaning, "a Buddha on their own"), consists of humans that have passed the learning phase and are now into continuing on their path of enlightenment through their own observations. Through their learning experiences in the previous realm, people in this realm have learned that they can only continue on their journey if they start to use what they've learned into the real world. They start to take learning to the next level as they begin to internalize what they've learned with the situations they find themselves in.

The third realm of nobility (ninth realm overall) is called the *Bodhisattva*. This realm is one of the highest realms a person can achieve. The people in this realm are the ones who want to continue to the realms of Buddhism so they can learn to become Buddhas themselves. At this point, they have reached their enlightenment, and now they are focusing on helping others to reach their enlightenment.

The people of this realm have become teachers and are ready to pass on their knowledge to eager learners.

The fourth realm of nobility (the final realm overall) is known as *Buddhahood.* This is the highest realm anyone can achieve. The people in this realm are often known as the enlightened ones and have such a high state of pure joy and compassion that nothing can bring them down. They have mastered the technique of Buddhist meditation and have an undeniable sense of peace within them that no one can shake.

In reality, it's rare that a person reaches the realm of Buddha, but it's not unheard of. Because the people of this realm have reached the highest level of compassion, understanding, and joy, it's not possible for them to fall back to any of the other nine realms. They will stay in this realm for the rest of their lives and focus their time and energy on trying to create a more compassionate and understanding world for others.

Hopefully, the ten realms of being have given you a better understanding of reincarnation in Buddhism. As stated before, if you're interested in learning about Buddhism and you're reading this book and other books on the topic, you are in the first realm of nobility. People in this realm generally spend their time learning through reading or talking to a guru who can help them better understand the points that they can't grasp. As you read on to the other realms, you've realized that learning just takes time, and by sitting in realm number 7, you're in a pretty good location as you're on your way to your enlightenment.

Nirvana

The best way to learn about nirvana when you're on your way to learning about Buddhism is to think of blowing out a flame. However, this isn't just any flame of a candle; you're blowing off the flame of your negative thoughts and emotions, such as greed, self-centeredness, jealousy, and hatred. In its place, you're lighting a new flame, one that holds the positive thoughts and emotions of compassion, peace, and spiritual joy. In a sense, nirvana holds the main goals of a Buddhist, which will lead you to your enlightenment. When you have reached nirvana, you have reached the ultimate goal for a Buddhist.

There are two states of nirvana. The first state is called the nirvana with the remainder. The second state of nirvana, the one that Buddha reached, is called the final nirvana.

Nirvana with a Remainder

This state of nirvana is the achievement of nirvana. This state occurs when the three fires, which are confusion, greed, and ill will, are no longer burning because you have blown them out. The reason why this state is referred to as nirvana with a remainder is that even though the three fires are out, there is one remainder, which people described as ashes or the five clinging-aggregates.

The five clinging-aggregates are described as the firewood that was used to keep the three flames burning. Now that they are out, it's no longer burning itself, but it's still there, and you can continue to see it as the remainder of the fires. In order to get rid of the remainder, you have to let go of the firewood. You won't reach the full state of nirvana with a remainder unless you let go of the firewood. Think of it this way—you had three people hurt you emotionally by starting a rumor that wasn't true. You believed these three people were your friends, but instead, they were just trying to get some information about you to start gossip. Because of their action, you stopped hanging out with them (blowing out the fires). However, your emotions over the situation (the ashes or the five clinging-aggregates) still remain. In order to truly let go of this situation and find peace, you need to get rid of the emotions you hold over the three people and the situation. Once you let go of these emotions, then you are officially able to feel nirvana.

Once you have completely let go of the firewood, you're no longer holding on to those negative emotions, and you're able to feel pure happiness and peace. Furthermore, you're able to continue to work toward reaching your enlightenment.

Final Nirvana

The final nirvana, also known as the nirvana without a remainder, is easy to figure out once you understand the nirvana with a reminder. This is the final nirvana. You can't go any farther than this, and it happens when the one who achieved the nirvana with a remainder passes on—meaning, they were able to let go of the ashes. In a sense, you can think of this as the Buddha's equivalent to heaven. This state of nirvana holds the idea that the person is no longer suffering from the physical world as they have died.

Chapter 7: Mindfulness and Meditation

Before you reach the state of enlightenment in Buddhism, you still have plenty of suffering caused by life events to see and face. In order to reach your enlightenment, it's important to know how to cope in these situations. If you're unable to cope, it'll be harder to reach your state of enlightenment. One of the most effective ways of relieving one's suffering and managing anxiety caused by life events is through what Buddhists call mindfulness meditation.

The term *mindfulness* means you pay close attention to the present—meaning, you live in the moment. When you combine this with meditation, you're able to get through the suffering and tough moments that life throws at you, and you can easily move on from them and continue to focus on your path of enlightenment.

In order to better explain the process of mindfulness meditation, I'm going to take a common life occurrence that's often a part of suffering, which is anxiety. So in this chapter, we're going to learn how to deal with anxiety through mindfulness meditation.

Overcome Anxiety through Mindfulness Meditation

Your Symptoms and Causes of Anxiety

In order to figure out what causes your anxiety and how you react to anxiety (meaning, your symptoms), you need to observe yourself in a state of anxiety. For example, when people feel anxious, they typically have both mental and physical systems. Their mental symptoms could be telling them that they are going to do poorly in something, like a test. On top of this, they can have physical symptoms of anxiety, such as rapid heartbeat, heavy breathing, and sweaty palms.

When you start to feel anxious, you need to observe where you are, what you're doing, or what you're about to do. Ask yourself, "Why are you becoming anxious?" Once you figure out the causes, you can move on to the next step, which is working on overcoming anxiety through mindfulness meditation. To give us an example of anxiety we can work on overcoming, let's take social anxiety.

In social anxiety, you become anxious when you have to talk to people or have to go out in a large group of people. Some people have social anxiety so bad that they literally do everything they can think of so they don't have to go outside of their comfort zone, which is normally their home or room. For this specific example, let's say we want to overcome the anxiety of being in a large crowd with our goal of being able to attend a concert we really want to go to.

Types of Mindfulness Meditation That Can Help You Overcome Anxiety

Now that we have figured out what causes our anxiety, which is being in large crowds, we can work on mindfulness meditation to help us overcome our anxiety so we can go to our concert.

One type of mindfulness meditation is called breathing meditation. This is generally one of the first techniques any therapist will advise you to learn when you're working on overcoming anxiety. That is because breathing techniques can be done anywhere, and people often don't realize that's what you're doing. However, instead of just using a breathing technique, we're going to do complete it in meditation form.

If you want to work on mindful breathing meditation to help get rid of your anxiety, you can do so by practicing deep breathing. There are several steps to this type of meditation.

Step 1: You want to find a location where you can lie or sit down comfortably. You can do this however you like, whether it's having your feet flat on the floor, sitting cross-legged on a cushion, or lying down on your back.

Step 2: Feel each regular breath as you're in your relaxed state. Pay attention to every movement.

Step 3: Now, you want to help yourself feel your natural breathing better, so you want to place one hand on your chest and the other on your stomach. Pay attention to the movements of your body as you breathe.

Step 4: Next, you want to form a rhythm with your breathing; but this time, you want to breathe deeply. With one hand still on your stomach and the other on your chest, start to breathe deeply slowly. As you inhale, you will notice your stomach rise, and as you exhale, you will notice it fall. During this process, you'll also notice that your chest keeps relatively still. You will also start to notice a rhythm as you continue to breathe deeply.

Step 5: With your rhythm going of deep breathing, you'll keep one hand on your chest and the other on your stomach. You want to continue deep breathing until you begin to feel calm and relaxed.

Whenever you feel anxious, whether it be from large crowds or anything else, you can use mindfulness meditation to ease your nerves. Over time, you won't have to think of the steps as you're meditating as it will become more natural. You will also begin to notice that you're less likely to become anxious over a certain situation the more you meditate.

Chapter 8: Buddhism and Science

Over the past few decades, Buddhism and science have started to work with each other. Scientists are looking more closely at the study of Buddhism to help understand and explain the universe as Buddhists are starting to use more scientific tools. One of the biggest reasons this has come to be is that science studies the mind and Buddhism focuses heavily on the mind. Of course, when it comes to science, one of the biggest studies of the mind lies within psychology.

Buddhism and Psychology

One of the biggest examples of how Buddhism and psychology work together is something we just discussed in the previous chapter, meditation. In psychology, one of the biggest therapies discussed when people are anxious or unable to deal with life's stressors is meditation and breathing exercises. Of course, there are many other techniques that psychologists focus on, but the two we discussed in the previous chapter are usually a therapist's go-to.

Another way Buddhism and psychology go together is Buddhism teaches that you need to remain positive, be compassionate, and remain calm in order to reach your enlightenment. While it's stated differently in the science of psychology, it holds the same beliefs. In psychology, there is a lot of talk about how people will have better self-esteem and feel overall better about themselves and their tasks at hand if they have a positive self-image and thoughts about themselves. Of course, like Buddhism, there is a fine line between having positive thoughts about yourself and becoming arrogant.

Dependent Origination

In Buddhism, dependent origination means that everything is connected. It means that if something happens, it is caused by something else, and this keeps going as one thing will always cause another thing. When it comes to science, this can often be compared to evolution. Through evolution, not only does human life continue to exists, but we have changed over time because of our surroundings—or as Buddhism would put it, because something happened to make us change.

Other Similarities

There are a few other similarities between science and Buddhism. One of these is that both studies believe that there isn't one creator of the universe that exists. Another similarity is both disciplines want to figure out how they can make things go easier and smoother for people. For example, they might wonder how they can help people or themselves understand time so they can understand life better. Just like science, Buddhism likes to focus on logic and reasoning.

Chapter 9: How Buddhism Can Help You in Your Daily Life

There are a variety of ways that Buddhism can help you in your daily life, which you're allowed to practice even if you aren't a Buddhist. This chapter will look at ways in which you can learn meditation and other techniques from Buddhism and bring them into your everyday life so you can also find your highest happiness and wisdom while living stress-free.

Anxiety

People from all over the world suffer from anxiety. Anxiety is described as fear about what is to come. It is a way of responding to stress. While some people have anxiety that's categorized as a disorder and need prescription medication in order to get a better handle of their anxiety, other people suffer more from situational-type anxiety. However, whatever type of anxiety you have, meditation can help calm you, which can lead you to have better control over anxiety and the situations that cause your anxiety.

One of the biggest techniques psychologists or therapists will teach you to manage your anxiety is to find activities that can help you relax. Some of the techniques that therapists usually recommend are breathing techniques, saying positive statements to yourself, and meditation.

Buddhists believe that meditation helps create a calmness within you, which gives you better control over your life. When you regularly take part in meditation exercises, you will slowly be able to gain better control of your anxiety.

Releasing Anger

People are often quick to come to anger. When we're angry, we not only say things that we don't generally mean, but we also can hold a grudge against someone. If this happens, we are more likely to not only speak negatively about the person but also let our anger cloud our minds and refuse to help them. We can also easily hurt someone whom we are angry at through various ways.

When you follow Buddha's teaching and perform meditation, you can start to release the anger inside of you as Buddhism teaches you to handle your anger skillfully. You will start to notice that you're much happier on the inside, which makes you happier on the outside. Through meditation and following many of Buddha's teachings, you'll learn to realize that anger isn't an emotion that we need to carry as it holds negativity. Instead, you will learn to not only remain calm, which will help control your anger, but also realize that anger won't solve anything and you're harming yourself when you become angry.

Making Compassion a Priority

This can tie into anger as, instead of becoming angry, you learn to have compassion toward people, including those who make you feel angry. One of the reasons that Buddhist teaching can help you make compassion for others a priority is that Buddhism teaches you to understand the world and the people around you better. When we start to understand people, we begin to release our anger. Once we release our anger, we start to have compassion for people.

The Five Precepts

Earlier in this book, we discussed the five main precepts that every Buddhist needs to follow, such as "Don't kill," "Don't steal," and "Don't consume alcohol or drugs." The five main precepts can easily help us in our everyday lives. When we listen to the first few precepts, such as "Don't kill" and "Don't steal," we are also listening to the laws, and following these precepts can help keep us out of prison.

People are human, and many are going to drink now and then, some more than others. However, anyone can follow the advice of Buddhists when they say that we shouldn't drink or take drugs because these things will cloud our mind. It is a scientific fact that drinking a certain amount of alcohol and taking certain drugs can cloud your mind. Not only can it make you believe that you're okay to drive home, but it can also make you do and say things that you usually wouldn't. On top of this, these things are often negative in nature, and Buddhists do their best to stay away from them because they want to remain calm, happy, and positive.

A Positive Outlook

A lot of Buddhist beliefs and practices talk about how you need to get yourself, especially your mind, to a positive outlook on life, or you won't be able to achieve your highest enlightenment. Having a positive outlook on your daily life can help by providing nearly the same achievement. When we have a positive outlook on ourselves and the things we do, we're more likely to succeed because we have the self-confidence and determination as we know we will do well in our task. When thinking about Buddhism, a great example of this is the task Buddhists go on so they can reach their highest point of enlightenment. If they didn't have a positive outlook, it would be harder for them to reach their level highest point of enlightenment. In fact, according to Buddha's teachings, it would be impossible to reach enlightenment as you can't reach enlightenment with negativity hanging over your head.

Conclusion

By now, you should have a better understanding of Buddhism than you did when you first picked up this book. Not only have I given a brief biography of the man who became Buddha, but we also discussed some of the basic beliefs of Buddhism and how to work toward your path of enlightenment. Through these basic beliefs and practices of Buddhism, you should be able to start walking down your path of enlightenment and begin techniques so you're able to provide yourself with a stress-free life. On top of this, through the beliefs and practices we discussed, you should be able to work toward a happier, wiser, and more fulfilling life of compassion, understanding, and positive self-care.

Because this is a book for beginners, I want to help you continue on your path of enlightenment by giving you more books you can look into from other beginner books that discuss different topics than I did in this book. I will also give more advanced reading materials for those who are interested in continuing on their path of enlightenment.

The Heart of the Buddha's Teaching: Transforming Suffering into Peace, Joy, and Liberation by Thich Nhat Hanh is a book that not only introduces us to the main teaching of Buddhism but also tells us how we can take these teachings and use them in our everyday lives.[1] Along with the Eightfold Path and the

---

[1] Hanh, T. (2015). *The Heart of the Buddha's Teaching: Transforming Suffering into Peace, Joy, and Liberation.* [online] Amazon.com. Available at: https://www.amazon.com/Heart-Buddhas-Teaching-Transforming-Liberation-ebook/dp/B011G3HD6I/ref=sr_1_4?crid=1HWG4G5A1NYXD&keywords=buddhism+for+beginners+book&qid=1550553045&s=gateway&sprefix=Buddhism%2Caps%2C426&sr=8-4.

Four Noble Truths, this book also discusses the Seven Factors of Awakening, Three Dharma Seals, and the Three Doors of Liberation.

If you like to learn about these things in a question-and-answer format, then Noah Rasheta's book *No-Nonsense Buddhism for Beginners: Clear Answers to Burning Questions about Core Buddhist Teachings* is one you should check out.[2] This book is stated to be very clear-cut, and it discusses the basics of Buddhism. Not only does the book answer some of the most common questions beginners of Buddhism have, but it also discusses some of the topics I touched on in this book, such as who Buddha is and what his teachings are. Written by a Buddhist teacher, this book is available in Kindle format on Amazon, and it is

---

[2] Rasheta, N. (2018). *No-Nonsense Buddhism for Beginners: Clear Answers to Burning Questions About Core Buddhist Teachings.* Kindle Edition.

for free if you have Kindle Unlimited.

Lawrence Wallace's book *Buddhism: Simplicity in a Distracted World: The Four Noble Truths and the Eightfold Path (Philosophy, Freedom, Zen, Advanced and Beginner Friendly Book 1)* is another beginner book that can help any aspiring Buddhist.[3] Wallace, who discusses beliefs and practices such as the Four Noble Truths and the Eightfold Path, does so in a way that is very easy for any beginner to follow.

In the book *In the Buddha's Words: An Anthology of Discourses from the Pali Canon (The Teachings of the Buddha)*, Bhikkhu Bodhi got together with His Holiness the Dalai Lama

---

[3] Wallace, L. (2017). *Buddhism: Simplicity in a Distracted World: The Four Noble Truths and the Eightfold Path (Philosophy, Freedom, Zen, Advanced and Beginner Friendly Book 1)*. Kindle Edition.

to bring forth this book.[4] Scholar and monk Bodhi put the book together, and the Dalai Lama gave the foreword. This is a great book for anyone, beginner or not, who is interested in or already part of Buddhism as it's one of the few books that is a collection of Buddha's teachings in his own words.

Of course, these are only a few of the books that are accessible on Amazon. There is also a lot of information on the internet through various web pages and books from Google Books.

No matter where your journey takes you from here, it's important to remember that the ultimate goal of Buddhism is to find everlasting peace. Once you find this peace, not only will you be able to think clearly, understand, and become full of compassion, but you will also be

---

[4] Bodhi (2005). *In the Buddha's Words: An Anthology of Discourses from the Pali Canon (The Teachings of the Buddha).* Kindle Edition.

able to keep your karma good, which will in return continue to give you good karma. If you're still unsure of where to start in your journey to find your true liberation, you can begin by clearing your mind for meditation. It's important to remember that as you begin meditation, you're not going to be perfect. There will be times that your mind wanders, and this is okay. You just need to catch yourself, and then you can start over, and before you know it, your meditation will become like second nature, and you won't have to worry about a wandering mind, at least not very often.

Bibliography

Bailey, M. (n.d.). *The 3 Principle Practices of the Buddhist Path.* Beliefnet.com. https://www.beliefnet.com/faiths/buddhism/articles/the-3-principle-practices-of-the-buddhist-path.aspx.

Bodhi. (2005). *In the Buddha's Words: An Anthology of Discourses from the Pali Canon (The Teachings of the Buddha).* Kindle Edition.

Buddhismforbeginners.com. (n.d.). *Buddhism for Beginners.* http://www.buddhismforbeginners.com/.

Budsas.org. (n.d.). *What Buddhists Believe: Precepts.* https://www.budsas.org/ebud/whatbudbeliev/161.htm.

Conze, E. (n.d.). *Five Precepts of Buddhism*

Explained. Tricycle: The Buddhist Review. https://tricycle.org/magazine/the-five-precepts/.

Fields, R. (n.d.). *Who Is the Buddha? The Story of Siddhartha Gautama*. Tricycle: The Buddhist Review. https://tricycle.org/magazine/who-was-buddha-2/.

Groove, B. (n.d.). *5 Ways of Integrating a Mindful Practice in Your Daily Life: Balance*. Balance. https://blog.buddhagroove.com/5-ways-of-integrating-a-mindful-practice-in-your-daily-life/.

Hanh, T. (2015). *The Heart of the Buddha's Teaching: Transforming Suffering into Peace, Joy, and Liberation*. Amazon.com. https://www.amazon.com/Heart-Buddhas-Teaching-Transforming-Liberation-ebook/dp/B011G3HD6I/ref=sr_1_4?crid=1H

WG4G5A1NYXD&keywords=buddhism+for+b
eginners+book&qid=1550553045&s=gateway&
sprefix=Buddhism%2Caps%2C426&sr=8-4.

Keown, D. (n.d.). *The Meaning of Nirvana in Buddhism Explained.* Tricycle: The Buddhist Review.
https://tricycle.org/magazine/nirvana-2/.

NewBuddhist (2010). "The 10 precepts . . . I'm just curious about some things."
http://newbuddhist.com/discussion/6311/the-10-precepts-im-just-curious-about-somethings.

O'Brien, B. (2018). *How Buddhism Agrees with Science.* ThoughtCo.
https://www.thoughtco.com/buddhism-and-science-449729.

Rahula, W. (n.d.). *The Noble Eightfold Path: Meaning and Practice.* Tricycle: The Buddhist Review.   https://tricycle.org/magazine/noble-eightfold-path/.

Rasheta, N. (2018). *No-Nonsense Buddhism for Beginners: Clear Answers to Burning Questions About Core Buddhist Teachings.* Kindle Edition.

Siv, S. *Buddhism: A Beginners Guide Book for True Self-Discovery and Living a Balanced and Peaceful Life: Learn to Live in the Now and Find Peace from Within.* Buddha/Buddhist Books by Sam Siv 1. Abundant Life LLC. Kindle Edition.

Terrell, S. (2018). *How To Practice Buddhism: A Guide for the Beginner Buddhist.* Mindvalley Blog. https://blog.mindvalley.com/how-to-practice-buddhism/?utm_source=google.

Tuhovsky, I. (2014). *Buddhism: Beginner's Guide: Bring Peace and Happiness to Your Everyday Life (Positive Psychology Coaching*

Series Book 5). Kindle Edition.

Unhcr.org (2012). *The Buddhist Core Values and Perspectives for Protection Challenges: Faith and Protection.* https://www.unhcr.org/50be10cb9.pdf.

Valentine, M. (n.d.). *7 Buddhist Teachings That Will Help You Overcome Life's Most Difficult Challenges and Find Peace.* Buddhaimonia. https://buddhaimonia.com/blog/7-buddhist-teachings-that-will-help-you-overcome-lifes-most-difficult-challenges-and-find-peace.

Wallace, L. (2017). *Buddhism: Simplicity in a Distracted World: The Four Noble Truths and the Eightfold Path (Philosophy, Freedom, Zen, Advanced and Beginner Friendly Book 1).* Kindle Edition.

Williams, M. (2014). *Buddhism: Beginner's Guide to Understanding & Practicing Buddhism to Become Stress and Anxiety Free (Buddhism for Beginners, Buddha, Zen Buddhism, Meditation for Beginners).* Kindle Edition.